9-11-19
$ 30.95

Diseases and Disorders of Youth

Kids and Cancer

Toney Allman

ReferencePoint Press®

San Diego, CA

© 2019 ReferencePoint Press, Inc.
Printed in the United States

For more information, contact:
ReferencePoint Press, Inc.
PO Box 27779
San Diego, CA 92198
www.ReferencePointPress.com

LIBRARY OF CONGRESS CATALOGING-IN-PUBLICATION DATA

Name: Allman, Toney, author.
Title: Kids and Cancer/by Toney Allman.
Description: San Diego, CA: ReferencePoint Press, Inc., 2019. | Series:
  Diseases and Disorders of Youth | Audience: Grade 9 to 12. | Includes
    bibliographical references and index.
Identifiers: LCCN 2017057235 (print) | LCCN 2017059051 (ebook) | ISBN
  9781682823989 (eBook) | ISBN 9781682823972 (hardback)
Subjects: LCSH: Cancer in children—Juvenile literature. | Cancer in
  adolescence—Juvenile literature.
Classification: LCC RC281.C4 (ebook) | LCC RC281.C4 A385 2019 (print) | DDC
  616.99/400835—dc23
LC record available at https://lccn.loc.gov/2017057235

Contents

A Once-Deadly Diagnosis

ancer is such a grave disease that, in the past, it threatened the life of every child it touched. But in 1955, at the National Cancer Institute in Bethesda, Maryland, the situation began to change. There, Dr. Emil Freireich and his medical team developed a treatment for the most common form of childhood leukemia, known as acute lymphoblastic leukemia (ALL). Leukemia is a cancer of the bone marrow—the tissue in the center of bones where blood cells are made. At the time of Freireich's research, ALL was 100 percent fatal. Freireich remembers, "The children would come in bleeding. They'd have infections. They would be in pain. Median survival was about eight weeks, and everyone was dead within the year."[1]

Freireich and his colleagues developed a combination of chemical substances, or chemotherapy, which involved four different drugs that, in high doses, destroyed cancerous cells and tissues. The drugs were highly toxic, or poisonous, not only to cancer cells and tissues but also to normal cells and tissues. Nevertheless, they were the only chance that children with leukemia had to survive. Between 1955 and 1965, children of all ages diagnosed with leukemia came to the hospital at the National Cancer Institute to be treated with the combination chemotherapy.

Toward Cures for Cancer

G. Bennett Humphrey was one of the doctors treating the children. No matter how sick they became or how severe the side effects were, his duty was to give each patient the toxic treatment for five days every month. Even when the cancer was in remission, the treatments did not stop. *Remission* means that the signs and symptoms of the cancer have disappeared, but all doctors know that remissions can be temporary. Cancer can hide in the body and reappear at any time. At that time, cancer in children usually returned within weeks or months. Therefore, the combination chemotherapy had to continue with the goal of killing all the cancer permanently.

The side effects of the treatment were severe and life threatening. Many children died despite the doctors' best efforts. Humphrey was often depressed and discouraged. He remembers thinking, "This is not why I went to med school. . . . Not to preside over death at the beginning of life."[2] Nevertheless, he and the other doctors at the National Cancer Institute continued to treat the children in their care, and they achieved the first cures of childhood leukemia. Fifteen percent of the children survived ten years—long enough to be considered a cure. It was not a huge success, but the combination chemotherapy treatment proved that childhood cancer was beatable. The medical community was set on the path of progress toward finding cures for all children with cancer. Medical scientists now believed that a cure was possible, and they intensified their efforts to find the right combination of new drugs and other treatments that would save the children.

Today medicine has come a long way. More than 80 percent of childhood cancers are either cured or achieve long-term remission, which is defined as five years of being cancer-free. Ninety

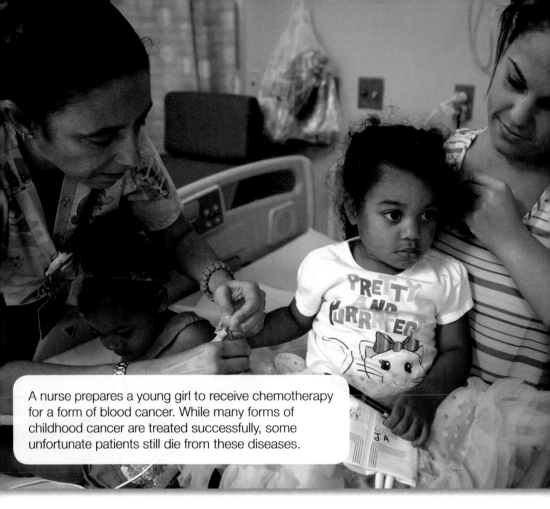

A nurse prepares a young girl to receive chemotherapy for a form of blood cancer. While many forms of childhood cancer are treated successfully, some unfortunate patients still die from these diseases.

percent of children with ALL reach this milestone. However, some children and young people still die of cancer. Many kinds of cancers exist, and some are more difficult to treat than others. Cancer continues to be a very grave disease.

When Cancer Strikes Kids

Cancer in young people is, however, rare. Worldwide, about 14 million people are diagnosed with cancer every year, but only about 300,000 of them are under age twenty. Most people who get cancer are older adults, but about 1 percent of the cancers diagnosed in the United States each year are found in children younger than fifteen years old—totaling about ten thousand kids. Another five thousand cases are diagnosed in teens aged fifteen through nineteen. In addition, for unknown reasons, cancer diagnoses in teens seem to be becoming more common. In 2017 researchers Jessica Burkhamer, David Kriebel, and Richard Clapp reported on their study of cancer in teens. They concluded, "We examined long-term incidence trends for ages 15–19 . . . and found that since 1975 overall cancer incidence increased by more than 25%."[3] Even though most of these cancers are survivable, that still means thousands of young people require long-term treatment, and about 600 teens die per year. An estimated 1,250 children under age fifteen die from cancer yearly in the United States as well.

Cancer research and treatment for young people remains an area of medicine that is ultimately about saving the lives of people who should have most of their lives ahead of them. That is why St. Jude Children's Research Hospital, which is devoted to cancer research and treatment, says, "We won't stop until no child dies of cancer."[4] Cancer is the leading cause of death from disease for children and teens, and a diagnosis of cancer is frightening. However, it is not at all the grim death sentence that it was in the past. In the fight against childhood and teen cancer, patients and doctors are winning.

> **"We won't stop until no child dies of cancer."[4]**
>
> —St. Jude Children's Research Hospital

What Is Cancer?

One bad cell is all it takes to set the process of cancer in motion. That single errant cell divides, multiplies, and continues to grow uncontrollably until it becomes a malignant mass of cells invading the body. The very definition of *cancer* is the uncontrolled growth of cells.

Cells and Cancer

The human body is made up of an estimated 37.2 trillion cells. Cells are the basic units of all living things. Each cell is a tiny, complex factory that produces the proteins that do the work of the body. Each cell in the body has its own specific function. Cells in the pancreas, for example, produce the insulin that is necessary for cells to use sugar for energy. Red blood cells carry oxygen to the body's cells. In every organ in the body, billions of cells work together and perform their specific functions as part of an elegantly organized system. When necessary to maintain organ and tissue health and growth, cells divide in a process called mitosis. The cell divides into two identical cells, and these daughter cells can divide again to make four, then eight, then sixteen cells, and so on. The process of cell division, however, is highly regulated by chemical signals within the cells. Each cell knows when to grow and when to stop growing. Cells are also chemically directed to die if they are damaged or defective, which is a process called apoptosis.

Cancer cells are rogue or renegade cells that do not follow the orderly processes of normal cells. Cancer cells proliferate, or multiply, rapidly and never turn off or die through apoptosis. As the American Association for Cancer Research explains, "Ignoring the body's signal to stop, malignant cells multiply to form tumors in organs and tissues or, in the case of blood cancers, crowd out normal cells in the blood stream and bone marrow."[5] Cancer cells are called *malignant* because they can invade and destroy nearby tissue and spread to other parts of the body. They steal nutrition from normal cells and can even cause the body to grow new blood vessels to bring oxygen and nutrients to the tumorous mass. Blood cancer cells simply become so abundant that there are not enough normal blood cells left to carry oxygen and nutrients to the rest of the cells in the body.

Although all cancers develop the same way, cancer is not just one disease—it is a collection of more than one hundred related diseases. Cancers are usually named for the organ or tissue in which they first arise. For example, brain cancer starts in the cells of the brain, and blood cancers may start in the cells of the bone marrow, where blood cells are produced. Even when the cancer cells travel to another part of the body, the type of cancer is determined by the organ where the disease first started. For instance, a tumor that forms in the brain may form its own blood vessels through which some cancer cells can escape to other parts of the body and start to grow. No matter what other organ may be affected by these breakaway cancer cells, the cancer is still considered a primary brain cancer. Some

> "Ignoring the body's signal to stop, malignant cells multiply to form tumors in organs and tissues or, in the case of blood cancers, crowd out normal cells in the blood stream and bone marrow."[5]
>
> —American Association for Cancer Research

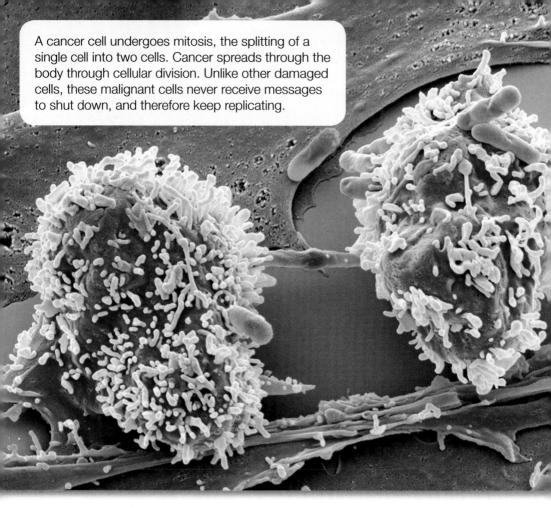

A cancer cell undergoes mitosis, the splitting of a single cell into two cells. Cancer spreads through the body through cellular division. Unlike other damaged cells, these malignant cells never receive messages to shut down, and therefore keep replicating.

common types of cancer include carcinomas, which are cancers of epithelial cells that line inner and outer body surfaces; sarcomas, which are cancers of bone, muscle, and other soft tissues; lymphomas, which are cancers of the lymphatic tissues that are part of the disease-fighting immune system; and leukemias, which attack white blood cells.

Leukemia

Some kinds of cancer are more common than others, and those that commonly occur in children and teens are different from those that occur in adults. The most common type in children and teens is leukemia, which accounts for about 30 percent of pediatric (childhood) cancers. Leukemia is cancer of the white blood cells. The most common type in young people is acute lymphocytic (lymph cell) leukemia (ALL), which accounts for about 75 percent of leukemias. The other common leukemia is acute myelogenous (bone-marrow-forming) leukemia (AML), and it accounts for most of the remaining leukemias. Both leukemias are called *acute* because they are fast growing. Both begin in the blood-forming cells in the centers of bones. New blood cells (such as red blood cells, white blood cells, and platelets for blood clotting) are made in the bone marrow by the master cells called stem cells. Stem cells are undifferentiated cells that can differentiate, or become, specific kinds of cells. In the bone marrow, these stem cells can become lymphocytes (white blood cells), myeloid cells (bone marrow cells), red blood cells, or platelets.

The white blood cells called lymphocytes are an important part of the immune system and fight infections. The two main types of lymphocytes are B cells, which make antibodies that signal the immune system that a germ has invaded, and T cells, which attack and kill invaders. ALL develops when one maturing lymphocyte—usually a B cell—is defective. Instead of developing into a normal B cell, the cancerous cell never matures completely. The immature cell is called a lymphoblast, and it does not perform the function of a white blood cell. It simply grows rapidly and multiplies.

AML also starts in the bone marrow, but it involves myeloid cells instead of lymphocytes. AML usually begins with a defective myeloid cell that should mature into a kind of white blood cell (other than a lymphocyte), but it can also start with a stem cell that is differentiating into a red blood cell or a platelet. As in ALL, the cancerous cells do not function correctly and crowd out normal cells. AML is also sometimes called acute myeloid leukemia or acute nonlymphocytic leukemia.

Leukemia cells build up so abundantly that the body does not have enough normal red blood cells, white blood cells, or platelets to maintain health. Without enough red blood cells, a person is anemic. The body is not getting enough oxygen to all the

11

cells and, as a result, the person can become weak, tired, dizzy, and short of breath. Without platelets to clot the blood, a person will bruise and bleed easily and suffer bleeding episodes, such as severe nosebleeds. Without enough of all the different kinds of white blood cells, a person gets frequent infections. Leukemia also causes bone and joint pain when the cancer cells build up near the surface of the bone or joint. Other symptoms include loss of appetite, weight loss, swollen liver and spleen, and headaches; with AML, rashes from leukemia cells also spread to the skin.

> **"When I was nine I began to feel very sick."[6]**
>
> —Ruben, leukemia patient

The symptoms of leukemia can occur with many other illnesses, and each individual can have a unique constellation of symptoms. Whereas some people feel unusually weak, others notice different problems. Thirteen-year-old Ruben, for example, remembers, "When I was nine I began to feel very sick. It began with my neck hurting to where I could not move it. Later the pain went down to my chest and ribs."[6] Ruben had ALL, for which he needed immediate treatment.

Solid Tumors of the Brain and Spinal Cord

Leukemia, as a cancer of the blood, does not form solid tumors, but the second most common form of childhood cancer does. About 26 percent of childhood cancers are brain and spinal cord tumors. These tumors are also among the most common cancers in teens. Several types of brain tumors have been identified, depending on where in the brain they originate and what kind of brain cells are involved. In general, though, they are masses of abnormal cells that can spread throughout the brain and spinal cord. Most such tumors in young people begin in the lower parts of the brain—in the cerebellum or the brain stem. No matter what part of the brain they affect, about half of all pediatric brain and spinal cord tumors are gliomas, meaning they start in glial cells. Glial cells surround and support the nerve cells, or neurons, in

Most Common Cancers in Children and Teens

Leukemia is the most commonly diagnosed cancer in children under the age of fourteen and epithelial cancers of the tissues lining surfaces of the body and organs are the mostly commonly diagnosed cancers in young people between the ages of fifteen and nineteen. This is the finding of a 2017 National Cancer Institute report. The pie charts show the incidence of different cancer diagnoses for children and teens worldwide between 2009 and 2012, which is the most recent information available.

Age-Adjusted and Age-Specific Cancer Incidence Rates for Patients Aged 0–14 Years, 2009–2012

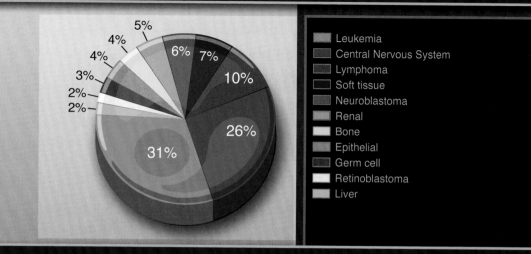

5%
4%
4%
3%
2%
2%
6%
7%
10%
26%
31%

- Leukemia
- Central Nervous System
- Lymphoma
- Soft tissue
- Neuroblastoma
- Renal
- Bone
- Epithelial
- Germ cell
- Retinoblastoma
- Liver

Age-Adjusted and Age-Specific Cancer Incidence Rates for Patients Aged 15–19 Years, 2009–2012

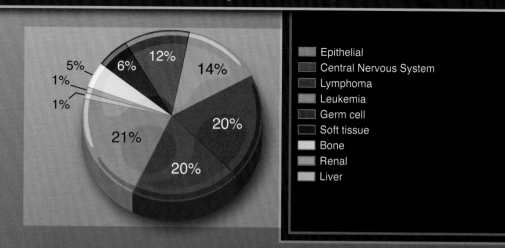

5%
1%
1%
6%
12%
14%
20%
20%
21%

- Epithelial
- Central Nervous System
- Lymphoma
- Leukemia
- Germ cell
- Soft tissue
- Bone
- Renal
- Liver

Source: National Cancer Institute, "Unusual Cancers of Childhood Treatment (PDQ®)–Health Professional Version," September 29, 2017. www.cancer.gov/types/childhood-cancers/hp/unusual-cancers-childhood-pdq.

the brain and spinal cord and are the most abundant cells in the central nervous system.

Symptoms of brain and spinal cord tumors vary according to where in the brain they occur and what parts of the brain are damaged or under pressure from the growing tumor. General symptoms can include headaches, dizziness, nausea and vomiting, seizures, and problems with balance. Tumors in the cerebellum, which controls physical coordination, can cause problems with walking, eating, and controlling movements. Tumors in the spinal cord can cause numbness and weakness in the arms and legs. Gliomas in the brain stem, which controls basic body functions such as breathing and wakefulness, can cause difficulty talking or swallowing and clumsiness in walking or using the arms and hands. They may also lead to droopy facial muscles and vision problems. When the tumor is in the cerebrum—the largest part of the brain, which controls thought, reasoning, emotions, and voluntary action—it can cause seizures, body weakness, changes in mood or personality, and changes in vision or hearing. Brain and spinal cord tumors can grow quickly, and the larger they become, the more surrounding healthy tissue is stressed and damaged.

Bone Sarcomas

Bone sarcomas are solid tumors. Sarcomas are cancers that originate in the cells of connective tissue, such as the cells in bone, cartilage, tendons, fat, and muscles. In children and teens, the most common type of bone sarcoma is osteosarcoma. Osteosarcoma is the third most common cancer in young people, and it affects more teens than children. Most of the young people who are diagnosed with osteosarcoma are between the ages of ten and twenty-four. This type of cancer accounts for about 2 percent of childhood and teen cancer; it affects about 450 young people a year.

Melanoma

Melanoma is an aggressive, fast-growing skin cancer that develops in the cells that produce melanin, the pigment that gives color to the skin. It is a serious kind of skin cancer because it so easily spreads, or metastasizes, to other parts of the body. Melanoma is extremely rare in children, but it is one of the most common cancers in teens. Approximately 7 percent of cancers in fifteen- to nineteen-year-olds are melanoma. The symptoms of melanoma can include a bump that is red or pale and itches or bleeds or a mole that is large, growing, or bleeding. When melanoma is diagnosed early, the treatment success rate is more than 90 percent.

Bone is living tissue that changes in structure as people grow from infancy to adulthood. In young people, some areas—called growth plates—are a mixture of bone and softer cartilage. The growth plates allow bones to lengthen as a child grows. Osteosarcomas tend to develop in the growth plates at the ends of the long bones in the arms and legs. About half of all bone tumors in children and teens originate at the end of the thigh bone (the femur) or at the end of the shin bone (tibia) that is closest to the knee. Sarcomas can also develop at the growth plate in the upper arm bone closest to the shoulder or in the pelvis, ribs, spine, or jaw. The most common symptom of a bone tumor is pain, with or without swelling, in the affected site. The pain may get worse with activity or at night. When it is in the leg bone, it may cause a person to limp or to be unable to move the knee joint freely.

Bone pain can be a symptom of many problems and injuries other than cancer, so it is sometimes difficult to know that something serious is going on. One mother whose daughter developed bone cancer remembers, "When Leeann was diagnosed with osteosarcoma in the left femur, I remember feeling total and utter shock. She had been complaining of pain in her knee for months, but since she was physically active playing basketball, baseball, and gymnastics, I assumed it was something minor like a pulled ligament. I also told her more than once that it was just 'growing pains.'"[7]

When medical examination identifies a bone sarcoma, about 20 percent of the time the cancer has already spread to a distant part of the body. This spread of cancer cells is called metastasis. Most commonly, osteosarcoma metastasizes to the lungs. Even when the cancer is present in the lungs, it is still considered osteosarcoma because the bone is the point of origin. Another way that osteosarcoma can spread is by occurring in multiple sites in the same bone where the cancer originated. These metastases are called skip lesions. Metastases are the reason that cancerous tumors are so dangerous. Some of the tumor cells break away and spread, eventually destroying tissues in other organs as well as the tissues where the tumor develops.

> "When Leeann was diagnosed with osteosarcoma in the left femur, I remember feeling total and utter shock."[7]
>
> —Mother of a child diagnosed with cancer

A rarer type of solid tumor bone cancer can also occur in young people. Affecting about 250 children and teens a year, the Ewing sarcoma family of tumors usually develops in the bones of ten- to twenty-year-olds. The cancer is named for James Ewing, the doctor who identified it in 1921. The tumors of Ewing sarcoma usually develop in the legs or pelvis. In rare instances, they can occur in the chest, skull, arms, hands, or spine. Pain and swelling at the site of the tumor is the most typical symptom. The Ewing sarcoma family of solid tumors differs from osteosarcoma in the way the cancer cells look under a microscope and because they are more easily killed with radiation.

Soft-Tissue Sarcomas

Not all sarcomas develop in bones. Soft-tissue sarcomas can also develop in children. The most common soft-tissue sarcoma in young people is called rhabdomyosarcoma (RMS), and it accounts for 3 percent of all childhood cancers. RMS usually starts in cells that develop into skeletal muscles, and the tumor can occur in almost any part of the body, including the abdomen, groin, head, neck, arm, or leg. About half of all RMS tumors occur in children younger than six years old, but older children and teens can be affected too. Whereas younger children are more likely to develop tumors in the head and neck, teens are more likely to develop them in the arms and legs. RMS also can grow in the genitals and urinary system at any age.

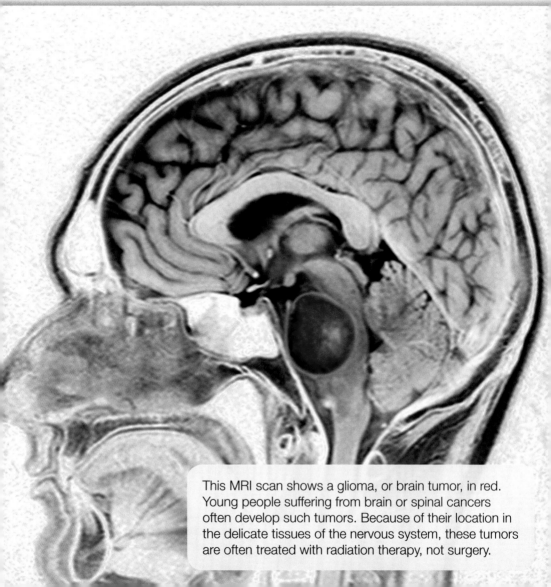

This MRI scan shows a glioma, or brain tumor, in red. Young people suffering from brain or spinal cancers often develop such tumors. Because of their location in the delicate tissues of the nervous system, these tumors are often treated with radiation therapy, not surgery.

The major symptom of RMS is a hard lump, or mass. It is not usually painful, but pain can occur if the tumor is pressing on certain tissues or nerves. One mother remembers discovering the lump on her son's body: "TJ was 2 ¾ when he came to me to help get his pants back up after using the bathroom. I saw one testicle was twice as large as the other and a darker color, almost purplish red. He said it didn't hurt."[8] Yet for Charlie, a sixteen-month-old boy, an RMS tumor caused serious abdominal pain. A tumor in his prostate (a gland between the bladder and the penis) grew so large that he was unable to urinate, causing his bladder to become painfully full. The tumor was discovered by doctors in the hospital. Charlie's mother explains that "they did an ultra-sound and an x-ray, and they saw a mass."[9]

Like a bone sarcoma, RMS can spread to other parts of the body, including to lymph nodes, lungs, bones, and bone marrow. Usually, the cancer cells spread first to nearby lymph nodes. (Hundreds of bean-shaped lymph nodes are located throughout the body, but they are most numerous in the neck, armpits, and

Emma and Neuroblastoma

Emma was one year old when she began to have symptoms of sickness. At first, she had a bad cough that would not go away. Then she began to sleep a lot and often refused to eat. She had fevers frequently and periodically vomited and had diarrhea. For a year, as her symptoms worsened, doctors thought Emma simply suffered from frequent infections, but then she began to have severe abdominal pains. At that point, a doctor found a lump in Emma's abdomen. A computed tomography scan revealed that the lump was a tumor over her right kidney. Finally, when Emma was two years old, she was diagnosed with neuroblastoma that had metastasized. Emma's life was in danger, and all that her mother, Samantha, could think was, "My little girl has cancer." Doctors gave the baby only a 20 percent chance of survival, but she has now been cancer-free for nine years.

Samantha, "Patient Stories: Emma's Story," Children with Cancer, July 2017. www.childrenwithcancer.org.uk.

groin.) Later, if the tumor remains undiagnosed, the cells can metastasize to distant parts of the body.

Other Common Cancers in Children

RMS disproportionately strikes young children, and some of the other most common pediatric cancers also are rare in older children and teens. Neuroblastoma, for example, is a solid tumor that accounts for about 6 percent of all childhood cancers, but it is rare in children older than ten. It usually develops in infants and very young children. More than 50 percent of neuroblastomas are found in children under two. It is a cancer of the nerve cells in the sympathetic nervous system. The sympathetic nervous system is a part of the peripheral nervous system that connects the central nervous system (the brain and spinal cord) to the limbs and organs of the body. It includes the adrenal glands that sit on top of the kidneys and produce hormones that help control heart rate, blood pressure, levels of sugar in the blood, and the ways that the body responds to strong emotions or stress, such as fear or excitement. Many neuroblastomas begin in the adrenal glands, but others develop in the nerve cells in the abdomen, on the kidneys, near the spine in the chest or neck, or in the pelvis.

Wilms tumor, which is a cancer of the kidneys, is another common pediatric cancer that almost always develops in young children. This cancer accounts for about 5 percent of childhood cancers and is typically found in three- to four-year-olds. Retinoblastoma is cancer of the eye and typically is found in children two years old or younger. It accounts for about 2 percent of childhood cancers. Young children can get other cancers too, such as liver cancer, but such cancers are quite rare.

Lymphoma and Teens

One type of cancer that is seen in teens but is uncommon in children is lymphoma. Lymphoma is more common in adults than in teens, but it is one of the most common cancers in fifteen- to nineteen-year-olds. It is not a solid tumor cancer. It is grouped with the blood cancers, but it begins in the lymphatic system. The lymphatic system is a network of thin tubes, lymph organs (such as the spleen and tonsils), and lymph nodes. It runs throughout the body and is an important part of the immune system, which fights diseases and protects the body from foreign invaders. The lymphatic system carries infection-fighting lymphocytes throughout the body. Lymphoma starts in the mature lymphocytes that congregate and multiply in the lymph nodes and other lymph tissues. When these lymphocytes become cancerous, they divide faster than normal lymphocytes do and live longer than they should.

There are two major types of lymphoma: Hodgkin lymphoma and non-Hodgkin lymphoma. In Hodgkin lymphoma, mature B cells become malignant. These cells have a characteristic appearance when viewed under a microscope that distinguishes them from the malignant cells of non-Hodgkin lymphoma, which can occur in either B cells or T cells. Hodgkin lymphoma is the type that most often affects older children and teens. It usually begins in a lymph node in the upper body, such as in the neck, chest, or armpits, and it spreads from lymph node to lymph node via the lymphatic system.

The main symptom of lymphoma is painless swelling in a lymph node. It is normal for lymph nodes to become tender and sore and to swell with white blood cells that multiply when the body is fighting an infection. By contrast, lymph nodes that are swollen from lymphoma contain defective, cancerous lymphocytes that are five times bigger than normal. Most of the white blood cells in the node are normal ones, but the huge cells cause the enlargement. No pain or tenderness is typically involved, and the enlarged node may grow bigger over time instead of going back to normal, as it would if an infection had gone away. Sometimes new lumps appear, either close to the swollen node or in other nodes in different parts of the body.

Other symptoms common with lymphoma include fever, extreme tiredness, weight loss, loss of appetite, and night sweats. If the affected lymph nodes are in the chest area, people may experience coughing, pain, and breathlessness as the enlarging node presses on the windpipe, or trachea. Lily, for example, was diagnosed with Hodgkin lymphoma when she was fourteen years old. She remembers how she felt before she knew what was wrong. She says, "I had unexplained chest pains for 8 months but put it down to muscular pains. But after a while I got more and more tired and then I lost a lot of weight and became deathly pale."[10] Although Lily's affected lymph nodes were in her chest, she did not suffer shortness of breath. As with all cancers, lymphoma symptoms vary with each individual.

Kids at Risk

No matter what their age, children and teens all face unique challenges when dealing with cancer of any kind. Whether the cancer is a solid tumor or a blood cancer, defective cells are growing out of control, causing serious symptoms and organ damage and putting lives at risk.

Chapter 2

What Causes Cancer?

When asked to relate the story of her cancer, thirteen-year-old Mary drew a series of pictures. In one picture, she drew a girl lying flat on a hospital bed. Tears stream down the girl's face. Underneath the drawing, Mary wrote only one large word: "Why!!!"[11]

That same question is asked by almost everyone who is touched by cancer—the young people diagnosed with the disease, their parents, their friends and siblings, and other loved ones. People wonder why cancer happened and often what they did wrong. One mother, Nancy Roach, remembers when her daughter Erin was diagnosed with cancer. She worried, "What had we done to cause this illness? Was I careful enough during pregnancy? . . . I wondered about the toxic glue used in my advertising work or the silk screen ink used in my artwork. Bob [Erin's father] questioned the fumes from some wood preservatives used in a project. We analyzed everything—food, fumes, and TV."[12]

Myths About Cancer

Much is still unknown about what causes cancer, but scientists do know what is not responsible. Nothing anyone did or did not do causes childhood or teen cancer. Many people, for instance, believe that lifestyle, especially diet, nutrition, and other health habits, play an important role in causing, preventing, or curing cancer in children and teens, but this is not true. As the American Cancer Society explains, "In adults, lifestyle-related risk factors, such as being overweight, eating an unhealthy diet, not getting enough exercise, and habits like smoking and drinking alcohol play a major role in many types of cancer. But lifestyle factors usually take many years to influence cancer risk, and they are not thought to play much of a role in childhood cancers."[13] Children and teens simply have not lived long enough for poor food choices or other bad habits to have had any effect on their chances of getting cancer.

> **"What had we done to cause this illness?"**[12]
>
> —Nancy Roach, the mother of a cancer patient

Researchers have attempted to determine whether a mother's diet or other health habits during pregnancy could increase her child's risk of developing cancer in early life; as yet, no firm evidence has been established. Some small studies have found links between the mother's diet and cancer, but other studies have not confirmed these results and find no evidence of such links. As Anne Spurgeon and Nancy Keene, pediatric cancer authorities and parents of childhood cancer survivors, say, "It may be difficult to accept, but parents need to understand that they did nothing to cause their child's illness."[14]

The National Cancer Institute (NCI) of the US Department of Health and Human Services describes some of the common myths about cancer and explains the scientific evidence that discredits these ideas. One myth is that eating a lot of sugar makes cancers grow and that eliminating sugar from the diet will make a cancer tumor shrink or disappear. Another is that artificial sweeteners can cause cancer. No scientific evidence exists for either idea. Despite many research studies, no link has been found between consuming sugar substitutes or sugar and cancer in people. Neither is cancer caused by cell phones, living close to electric power lines, exposure to the chemicals in hair dyes or deodorants, or fluoride in drinking water or toothpaste. All of these factors have been suggested at one time or another as increasing the risk of cancer in people. Some alternative medical practitioners do believe that such factors can play a role in cancer development. The NCI, however, maintains that no standard scientific studies have yet supported an association between these factors and cancer.

> "It may be difficult to accept, but parents need to understand that they did nothing to cause their child's illness."[14]
>
> —Experts Anne Spurgeon and Nancy Keene

Finally, the NCI explains that contrary to what some people fear, cancer is not infectious or contagious. No one catches cancer from another person, and no one with cancer can give it to anyone else. The institute states that "wrong ideas about cancer can lead to needless worry"[15] and offers information as opposed to myths and false ideas. It also explains what is known about the cause of cancer. According to the NCI, "Cancer is a genetic disease—that is, cancer is caused by certain changes to genes that control the way our cells function, especially how they grow and divide."[16]

Genes and How They Work

The nucleus, which is located in the center of almost every cell in the body, contains genes that determine how each cell functions. Each cell of the human body has about twenty thousand to twenty-five thousand genes. In humans, these genes are grouped into twenty-three pairs of chromosomes. Each chromosome is made up of two strands of deoxyribonucleic acid (DNA) arranged as a spiraled, coiling ladder. DNA carries the complete genetic code for constructing the body by directing the construction of proteins. Scientists explain that the DNA code is like a giant book, and all the sentences in this book form the whole human genome (the complete set of genes). The genetic letters of this book can be thought of as a chemical alphabet. The rungs, or bases, of the DNA ladder are the chemicals that form the instructional code of the alphabet. Four letters make up this alphabet. They are A (the chemical adenine), T (thymine), G (guanine), and C (cytosine). At each rung, A can join only with T to make a base pair, and C bonds with G. There are about 3 billion letters in the human genome. These letters form the so-called chemical words that are always written in groups of three and carry the instructional code for a cell's function. These three-letter words are called codons.

Although almost every cell contains the body's complete DNA code in its nucleus, most of the instructions are turned off. All of the cells function together in a complex network, and each cell uses only the pertinent DNA instructions to perform its own function. For example, a muscle cell, grouped with many other muscle

Some people believe cancer can be caused by cell phones or living too close to power lines. However, many scientists maintain that no credible evidence exists to verify a cause-and-effect connection.

cells, follows the DNA instructions to perform its normal muscle function. It does not use the DNA instructions for bone or brain cells.

DNA spells out the genetic instructions, but it does not actually make the cell's proteins. That is the job of ribonucleic acid (RNA). RNA is the transfer and messenger system of the cell. It reads the DNA instructions, and this information tells the cell what protein to manufacture. For example, the DNA codon TTT calls for the manufacture of the chemical phenylalanine, an amino acid that is one building block of a protein. It takes many codons in a specific order, or sequence, to form the instructions to make a protein. This long string of codons is like words in a sentence.

Cancer and Twins

Scientists continue to engage in medical research with the goal of identifying any possible risk factors associated with childhood cancer. The ultimate hope is to use this knowledge of risk factors to prevent cancer in children. One approach to this research is to examine identical twins. Identical twins share almost the same genes; therefore, if a gene is responsible for a disease, both twins should contract it. In several studies, researchers have questioned whether one child being diagnosed with cancer means that the other will get cancer too. Scientists have determined that if one twin is diagnosed with leukemia before the age of six, there is an increased risk that the other will have leukemia. However, that risk is only 20 percent. Researchers speculate that gene mutations that lead to leukemia must occur while the infants are developing in the uterus. Sometimes, both identical twins are affected, but not always.

In one case, one identical twin girl developed leukemia at age two. She had a specific gene mutation known to increase the risk of leukemia. Her sister did as well, but she did not develop cancer. Scientists can only speculate about why one twin got leukemia and the other did not. They hypothesize that additional acquired mutations led to the development of cancer in the first child that did not occur in the second. Researchers have a long way to go before they fully understand how acquired mutations cause cancer and which ones and how many must mutate for cancer to result.

These words and how they are arranged in the sentence make up a gene. RNA reads and translates this code and directs the cell to produce its protein. Each gene carries instructions that tell RNA where to start reading the code and where to stop.

Genetic Variations and Mistakes

A gene is a specific string of DNA that is the basic unit of inheritance. It chemically codes for traits, which are determined by the protein a cell manufactures. Chromosomes (and their genes) are passed from parents to offspring, with one of each pair inherited from the mother and the other from the father. That is why children inherit certain traits, such as eye color or height, from their parents, and it is also why the tendency to inherit certain diseases can be passed down in families.

More than 99.9 percent of the DNA in all humans is the same. The genes are the same and are arranged in the same sequences on the DNA ladder. It is the 0.1 percent differences in genetic codes that make each person a unique individual. Scientists estimate that in each gene, one to three bases (or rungs on the ladder) are different for every person. These differences can make people unique by changing the way a cell makes a protein, how much protein it makes, and how the protein functions. Most differences in genes are normal variations and do no harm. Normal variations, such as differences in eye color, are called alleles. These genetic variations have been there ever since the person was a fertilized egg—a zygote—and are built into every gene in the body. They are passed from parents to children.

Mutations are similar to variations; both are changes in the DNA sequences of a gene. Scientists say that these changes are like misprints in the letters that make up the sentence that is the gene. Mutations are mistakes in the DNA code. Two main types of mutations exist—inherited and acquired. An inherited mutation is one that was present in the parental egg or sperm that formed the zygote and then the developing fetus and the child. It is present

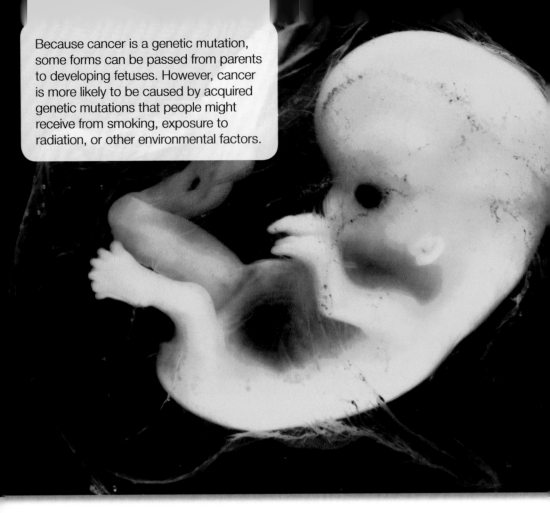

Because cancer is a genetic mutation, some forms can be passed from parents to developing fetuses. However, cancer is more likely to be caused by acquired genetic mutations that people might receive from smoking, exposure to radiation, or other environmental factors.

in the nucleus of every cell in the body, and it can be passed on to that individual's offspring in the future. Some diseases, such as cystic fibrosis, are caused by mutations like this. Small changes in the base pairs of a certain gene cause the person to be born with the disease. Such inherited diseases are uncommon.

The most common mutations are acquired mutations. Acquired mutations are not present in the zygote, do not appear in every cell in the body, and cannot be passed down in families. They are mutations that occurred sometime after the zygote was formed and affect only some cells in the body. More than 95 percent of the time, cancer is caused by acquired mutations. Therefore, when scientists say that cancer is a genetic disease, they do not mean that the disease was inherited. They are referring to the DNA mutations that were acquired by certain cells, causing the cancer to begin. These mutations are sometimes referred to as *somatic*, meaning "related to the body."

The Environment and Cancer

Acquired mutations can occur for many reasons. In adults, mutated genes commonly come from exposure to events that do damage to the genes over a lifetime. For example, decades of smoking cigarettes gradually damage enough genes in the lungs to alter the DNA instructions in the cells. Another type of exposure that can damage genes is radiation from some sources. These include radiation from the sun, which can cause skin cancer; high levels of exposure to the natural gas radon, which is found in soil and rocks and can affect lung cells; and repeated exposure to X-rays or to radiation-producing uranium, such as in uranium mines. Nuclear power plant accidents, such as the 1986 Chernobyl disaster in the former Soviet Union, can produce so much radiation that people experience cell damage. People who survived the atomic bombings in Hiroshima and Nagasaki, Japan, also suffered mutated genes. The radiation actually breaks the base pairs on the DNA ladder.

Other environmental causes of genetic damage in adults include poor nutrition, which slowly damages cells over time, and some hormones. Hormones are chemicals produced by the body to regulate organs and tissues. They play a role in controlling cell division. Artificially made hormones in high doses can increase cancer risk over time.

Exposure to carcinogens—substances capable of causing cancer—can be an important factor in why adults develop cancer. However, even most cancers in adults are not caused by carcinogens. And except for rare instances of radiation exposure during nuclear events, no carcinogens have been identified for the cancers that develop in children and teens. When young people are exposed to carcinogens, the risk of developing cancer decades later, especially with repeated exposures, does increase, but no sunburn, no exposure to cigarette smoke, no breathing of chemicals, and no food choices can give a child or teen cancer at their stage of life. The slow changes to genes caused by carcinogens have not had enough time to occur. The environment, therefore, seems to have nothing to do with why young people get cancer.

Random Genetic Accidents and Cancer

Cancer often seems to start with randomly acquired mutations that occur during cell division, when cells are multiplying. Cell division maintains the health and growth of the body. Old or damaged cells are continually being replaced by new ones, and young bodies grow larger through cell division. Cells divide by first growing larger, duplicating the chromosomes in the nucleus, and then splitting into two identical daughter cells. The duplication of chromosomes is usually accomplished perfectly, but not always. Sometimes, mistakes can creep in. Changes that are similar to typos can occur that alter the DNA in a gene. Sometimes, a chemical letter is omitted, an extra letter is added, or a letter is substituted for another. As the American Cancer Society explains,

> "Every time a cell divides, it is another opportunity for mutations to occur."[17]
>
> —American Cancer Society

> Every time a cell divides, it is another opportunity for mutations to occur. . . . It is important to realize that gene mutations happen in our cells all the time. Usually, the cell detects the change and repairs it. If it can't be repaired, the cell will get a signal telling it to die in a process called apoptosis. But if the cell doesn't die and the mutation is not repaired, it may lead to a person developing cancer.[17]

Reading Gene Sentences

The Genetic Science Learning Center at the University of Utah explains how genes code instructions. A genetic code is like a sentence made up of three-letter words. The center gives an example of this sentence (in English instead of the DNA letters ACTG): "Thesunwashotbuttheoldmandidnotgethishat." When the sentence is split into three-letter words, it makes sense: "The sun was hot but the old man did not get his hat."

The center explains that "this sentence represents a gene. Each letter corresponds to a nucleotide base, and each word represents a codon." But if an extra letter (a mutation) is thrown into the sentence, it can no longer be read correctly. As an example, an extra *s* may be added after the word *was*. When split into groups of three-letter words, the sentence now reads, "The sun was **s**ho tbu tth eol dma ndi dno tge thi sha t." Nothing makes sense anymore. This is what happens when a mutation occurs in a gene and its DNA. The code is no longer read correctly, the proper protein is not made, and disease can result.

Genetic Science Learning Center, "How Do Cells Read Genes?," March 1, 2016. http://learn.genetics.utah.edu.

Acquired mutations and damaged DNA often are a normal part of life that do no harm, but there are two main types of genes in which mutations may lead to cancer. The first type is named proto-oncogenes. Proto-oncogenes are normal genes that code for proteins that stimulate the cell to divide and prevent cell death. They also help stop a cell from differentiating, or becoming a fully formed, specialized cell. Proto-oncogenes turn on, or activate, only when needed to protect normal cell functions. If a proto-oncogene mutates, however, it may stay activated all the time. It may prevent the cell from dying even though the cell is malfunctioning. It becomes an oncogene—a gene that may cause the cell to grow out of control. (*Onco* is Greek and means "tumor" or "mass.") Oncogenes, wherever they occur in the body, can lead to cancer. Scientists are able to read the full DNA code of cancer

31

genes in a process called genomic sequencing and have identified more than one hundred different oncogenes with varying mutations that cause different kinds of cancer.

Tumor suppressor genes are the other major type of genes that may, when damaged, lead to cancer. When they are functioning normally, tumor suppressor genes slow down cell growth, repair any DNA mistakes, and signal cells when it is time to die through apoptosis. When mutations cause tumor suppressor genes to malfunction, they may be inactivated and fail to prevent cell growth. They also can fail to repair DNA mistakes and fail to tell the damaged cell to die. The American Cancer Society says that "a tumor suppressor gene is like the brake pedal on a car. It normally keeps the cell from dividing too quickly, just as a brake keeps a car from going too fast. When something goes wrong with the gene, such as a mutation, cell division can get out of control."[18] One tumor suppressor gene, which scientists have named TP53, has been found to be mutated in more than half of all human cancers.

Mutations and Cancer in Young People

Just as in adults, most cancers in children and teens are believed to be caused by mutations in genes. Less than 5 percent of the time, these mutations are inherited. For example, about 10 to 20 percent of the young children with retinoblastoma (a rare cancer of the eye) inherited the mutated gene from a parent. The tumor suppressor gene RB1 is defective, and the child is born with a mutation that causes the cancer in both eyes. Because the mutated gene is inherited, it is in every cell of the child's body, and the normal RB1 gene inherited from the other parent was damaged as the child's eyes developed. Usually, however, mutations in the RB1 gene are acquired; they do not appear in every body cell, and the child has the tumor in one eye only. These mutations are accidents with no known cause.

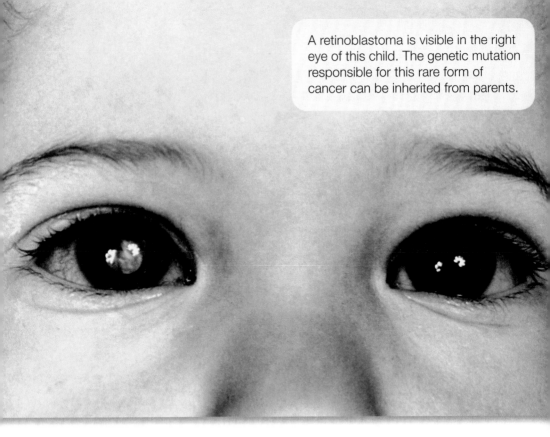

A retinoblastoma is visible in the right eye of this child. The genetic mutation responsible for this rare form of cancer can be inherited from parents.

At least 95 percent of the time, cancers are caused by acquired mutations. Some of these mutations are acquired before the child is even born, while he or she is still developing in the mother's uterus. Others seem to occur later in childhood or adolescence. Mutations in a single gene are sometimes enough for cancer to develop, but most of the time the disease requires several mutated genes. In addition, some forms of childhood and teen cancers are caused by mutations in different locations on a single gene.

With acute lymphoblastic leukemia (ALL), for instance, different subtypes of the disease have been identified, along with dozens of possible mutations. In some cases, the gene IKZF1 has deletion mutations—some bases on the DNA ladder have been omitted. In other instances, the genes known as NRAS, FLT3, JAK3, and IL7R were mutated. One mutation that is rare in children but common in adults is called the Philadelphia chromosome (named for where it was discovered), in which two genes—BCR and ABL—on the same chromosome are fused together. Commonly, genetic material also may be exchanged between chromosomes. This kind of mutation is called a chromosome translocation. Often the TEL gene, which belongs on chromosome 12, has been translocated next to the AML1 gene on chromosome 21. Such exchanges affect the functioning of the cell and how it makes proteins; with ALL, the mutations prevent the B cells in the bone marrow from developing normally.

With other cancers in children and teens, less is known about possible mutations. For instance, in Wilms tumor (cancer of the kidney in children), all of the genetic mutations responsible have yet to be identified. Some of the time, alterations or deletions of specific tumor suppressor genes are found; in the majority of children, however, these changes are not found. That fact tells researchers that multiple genetic mutations are responsible for the tumor, but which ones they are and how they work together to cause the cancer is still unknown.

Still Unraveling the Medical Mystery

The many different mutations that can give rise to cancer in children and teens mean that cancer is an extremely complex disease that is difficult to understand and explain. The genetic mutations do not occur in every cell in the body. They are mutations in the cancerous cells themselves, and all the other body cells have perfectly normal genes. Medical researchers continue to search for the factors that might cause certain genes to mutate and cells to become cancerous, but so far they have few answers. That means that the medical world does not know how to prevent childhood and teen cancer either. The first step is identifying the genetic mutations that lead to all cancers, with the goal of figuring out why these changes occur and how best to treat each young person's cancer.

St. Jude Children's Research Hospital, for instance, is dedicated to treating childhood cancer. A major area of the hospital's research is determining cancer's genetics. According to St. Jude, "The roots of pediatric cancer are hidden deep within a child's DNA. The St. Jude–Washington University Pediatric Cancer Genome Project is the world's most ambitious effort to discover the origins of childhood cancer and seek new cures."[19] If this project and others around the world are successful, scientists will know the DNA structure of every cancerous cell. They will not only be able to explain the origins of cancer but also will be closer to conquering it. Until that time comes, however, there is no ultimate explanation for the cause of cancer.

Chapter 3

Can Cancer Be Treated or Cured?

Modern medicine offers treatment options for all childhood and teen cancers. The success rate of treatment depends on the type of cancer, how much the cancer has grown and spread, and how quickly the cancer responds to treatment. As the Children's Cancer Institute in Australia explains, "Every child is unique, every cancer is different, so the cure has to be targeted for each individual."[20] Today, more than 80 percent of young people treated for cancer are alive five years after diagnosis.

Treatment Goals and Plans

Most doctors consider five years cancer-free to be a milestone. If a young person has no signs or symptoms of cancer for five years after treatment, he or she is considered cured. Before that time, when a person has finished treatment and shows no evidence of disease, doctors say the person is in remission. Remission means that no cancer cells can be found, but doctors are not sure whether cancer cells are hiding in the body. If they are, the cancer may start growing again, and the person may relapse and need more treatment. Relapses usually occur within the first three years after treatment. Thus, the more years that have passed, the more likely the cancer is gone for good. Often, even cancer that relapses can be treated again and eventually cured. Most children diagnosed with leukemia, for instance, are cured and live long, healthy lives, but other cancers are more aggressive and harder to treat. Modern cancer research is ongoing and intense, with the goal of developing new treatments to ensure that every child and teen survives cancer, no matter how aggressive it is.

Cancer is a serious disease, and the treatment must be powerful and rigorous. Most children are treated in specialized children's cancer centers, where teams of experts can provide the most up-to-date treatments and understand the unique needs of their patients. These experts include pediatric oncologists (childhood cancer specialists), pediatric surgeons (surgeons who specialize in surgery for children), pediatric oncology nurses, and physical therapists, psychologists, and nutritionists who have expertise in cancer care for children. Several other medical specialists are commonly part of the team as well. Teens, too, are often treated in these centers because their cancers typically are more similar to childhood cancers than to adult cancers.

Treatment usually begins immediately after diagnosis. Standard treatment protocols (or plans) have been developed for every kind of cancer. The treatment protocol is the best treatment that has been determined by medical science to work for the most young people with that particular kind of cancer. Each protocol usually includes several different treatment approaches. The main treatments available (depending on the cancer) are chemotherapy, radiation therapy, surgery, and stem cell transplantation. With some cancers, doctors are also using targeted therapy, which attacks specific kinds of cancer cells, and immunotherapy, which uses the immune system to fight cancer cells. Not every person gets every kind of treatment, but each individual gets the combination of treatments most likely to kill his or her cancer and lead to a cure.

How Childhood Cancer Survival Has Improved

Childhood cancer survival dramatically increased in England between 1990 and 2015, according to statistics published in 2017. In 1990, about 65 percent of all children with cancer survived for at least ten years. By 2015, that number had improved to 80 to 85 percent overall. At all age levels, today's treatment methods have led to improved outcomes and more cures.

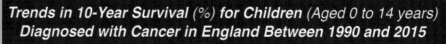

Trends in 10-Year Survival *(%)* **for Children** *(Aged 0 to 14 years)* **Diagnosed with Cancer in England Between 1990 and 2015**

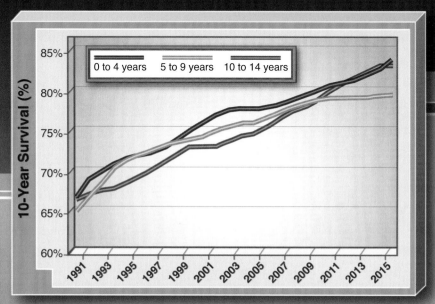

Source: More Trials.net, "Treatment of Childhood Cancer in the UK: A Learning Healthcare System in Action," September 29, 2017. http://moretrials.net.

Chemotherapy

Almost everyone with cancer receives chemotherapy. Chemotherapy, or chemo, is treatment that uses chemicals—medicines or drugs—to damage cancer cells and prevent them from reproducing through cell division. More than one hundred chemotherapy drugs are used in cancer treatment, and several are typically part of the protocol. These drugs may be used together, but more often they are administered at different times during treatment, which may last two or three years. The combination is necessary because different chemo drugs attack cancer cells in slightly different ways. Some, for instance, damage cancer cells by breaking down the cell walls. Others damage a cell's DNA so that it cannot divide. Still others starve cancer cells by blocking them from receiving cell nutrients needed for growth. Since cancer cells grow and reproduce more rapidly than normal cells, chemotherapy generally works by slowing and stopping cell division.

Chemo is typically given through an intravenous (IV) line, so that the drug can drip into the vein and be carried throughout the body. Doctors commonly implant an IV catheter, or port, during a minor surgical procedure. The catheter tube is inserted into a large vein in the chest or upper arm. With this apparatus, chemo patients can easily receive IV medicines without having to be injected with additional needles.

When formulating a chemo treatment plan, doctors consider the type of cancer involved, how fast it is growing, and whether it is likely to metastasize. These factors will determine which drugs are used, their strength, and how long they must be taken. With acute lymphoblastic leukemia (ALL), for instance, the standard chemotherapy treatment plan includes three steps. The National Cancer Institute explains:

The treatment of childhood ALL is done in phases:

- Remission induction: This is the first phase of treatment. The goal is to kill the leukemia cells in the blood and bone marrow. This puts the leukemia into remission.

- Consolidation/intensification: This is the second phase of treatment. It begins once the leukemia is in remission. The goal of consolidation/intensification therapy is to kill any leukemia cells that remain in the body and may cause a relapse.

- Maintenance: This is the third phase of treatment. The goal is to kill any remaining leukemia cells that may re-grow and cause a relapse. Often the cancer treatments are given in lower doses than those used during the remission induction and consolidation/intensification phases.[21]

Commonly, chemotherapy treatment for young people is intensive and involves high doses of drugs. Cancer in children and teens tends to be aggressive and multiply rapidly, and that means the cancer cells are more easily killed than those in adults. The American Cancer Society says that "there are exceptions, but childhood cancers usually respond well to chemotherapy because they tend to be cancers that grow fast. . . . Children's bodies are also generally better able to recover from higher doses of chemotherapy than are adults' bodies."[22] Older teens, however, may not be able to recover as quickly as young children can.

> "There are exceptions, but childhood cancers usually respond well to chemotherapy because they tend to be cancers that grow fast."[22]
>
> —American Cancer Society

Chemo and Side Effects

Coping with the side effects of chemotherapy, however, is not easy for anyone. Chemo is basically a toxin—a poison—and it can have harsh physical effects. Some normal, healthy cells in the body are relatively fast growing too, and when chemo damages cancer cells, it also poisons those cells. This can mean difficult side effects—undesirable consequences of the treatment. Doctors have to balance the dosage necessary to kill the cancer cells against the risk of harming the patient. Healthy body cells that grow quickly include hair cells, bone marrow cells, skin cells,

Saved by His Sister

When Bradley Godish was four years old in 2014, he was diagnosed with acute myeloid leukemia. He was treated for four months with high doses of chemotherapy, but the therapy failed to cure his cancer. At that point, doctors decided that the best way to save his life was through a stem cell transplant. Bradley's mother, Jennifer Godish, remembers, "Luckily, Bradley's twin sister and sidekick, Charlie, was a perfect match for him. Charlie donated her stem cells to her brother on February 17, 2015, and he remained in the hospital for almost a month in order to recover. But thanks to Charlie's super fighter cells, Bradley has a new chance at life." By February 2017, Bradley was still in remission and doing well. There was no sign of cancer, and his immune system cells were functioning normally.

Jennifer Godish, "Bradley Godish, Acute Myeloid Leukemia: 4 Years Old at Diagnosis," CureSearch, January 11, 2017. https://curesearch.org.

and the cells lining the mouth, stomach, and intestinal tract. This is why, for example, people undergoing chemo usually lose their hair. Clarissa Schilstra had ALL as a young child, and it relapsed when she was thirteen years old. She lost her hair several times during the two and a half years that she was treated for the relapse. She remembers,

> The scariest part of that first experience with hair loss was waking up in the morning and finding more hair on your pillow than on your head. . . . When you lose your hair, it is no longer possible to ignore the fact that you have cancer and you are forced to confront it. Even worse, you are forced to confront the fact that, in order to live, you must let the medicines essentially destroy your body inside and out.[23]

Other side effects from chemo can include painful mouth sores, skin rashes, diarrhea, nausea and vomiting, and extreme fatigue and weakness—all a result of damage to fast-growing normal cells. When people are receiving chemo, doctors pre-scribe antiemetics to prevent vomiting, antidiarrheal medications, ointments for skin rashes, and bland diets that are easy to digest.

Sometimes, so many healthy red blood cells are damaged that the chemo patient becomes anemic and needs a blood transfu-sion. Likewise, extensive damage to healthy white blood cells can prevent the person's body from fighting infections. Thus, chemo patients with very low white blood cell counts may have to wear face masks so they do not breathe in germs that others may be carrying. They and everyone around them must wash their hands frequently and thoroughly. They may have to avoid public places, stay out of school, and eliminate contact with friends until the white blood cells in their bodies begin to recover.

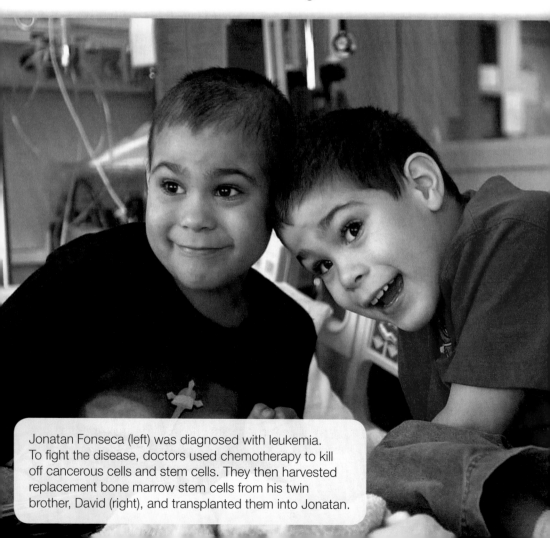

Jonatan Fonseca (left) was diagnosed with leukemia. To fight the disease, doctors used chemotherapy to kill off cancerous cells and stem cells. They then harvested replacement bone marrow stem cells from his twin brother, David (right), and transplanted them into Jonatan.

Fortunately, side effects disappear once treatment is completed. Hair grows back, blood counts recover, and stomach and intestinal issues fade away. But not everyone gets serious side effects from chemo. Some young people have little difficulty, and some get only a few side effects or react to only one of the chemo drugs while doing well with others. Each patient is an individual whose body reacts in individual ways to the treatment. Chemo is usually given in cycles, with one round of chemo, then a break, and then another round with the same or a different drug. Frequent blood testing and examinations of cells tell the medical team when the treatment can be completed because the cancer is in remission.

Stem Cell Transplantation

Sometimes, chemo is not enough for treatment to be successful. In neuroblastoma, for example, the very high doses of chemo necessary to kill the tumor cells also make it impossible for the stem cells in the bone marrow to survive. Medical researchers have determined that the best treatment protocol in these cases includes stem cell transplantation. With this procedure, doctors harvest the child's stem cells from the blood or bone marrow and preserve them. Then the child receives high-dose chemotherapy that kills as many tumor cells as possible. The child's stem cells also die, but the previously harvested stem cells are then transplanted, or infused, back into the veins. From there, the stem cells migrate to the bone marrow and begin producing new, healthy blood cells. Doctors can store enough stem cells to repeat this procedure if further intensive chemo treatments are needed to destroy the tumor. Today the standard protocol for children with aggressive neuroblastoma includes stem cell transplantation.

Stem cell transplants are sometimes a treatment for leukemia as well. Children with ALL, for example, who have the Philadelphia chromosome in which two genes are fused together, may need a stem cell transplant. Children whose leukemia relapses soon after treatment or who have been treated twice unsuccessfully with chemo alone may need a transplant. However, since their cancer is in their stem cells, doctors cannot use the patient's own stem cells for the transplant. They need cancer-free stem cells from a donor. Donor cells must be a good match for the patient, just as donated blood types have to match that of the person receiving a blood transfusion. Often, a child's sibling is a good match and can donate stem cells. In this procedure, the young person is given such high-dose chemotherapy that his or her bone marrow is destroyed. Afterwards, the donor stem cells are transplanted into the chemo patient's body, where they grow in the bone marrow and produce healthy blood cells.

Radiation Therapy

When chemotherapy is not enough to destroy cancer, radiation may also be used, especially for solid tumors. Typically, radiation therapy involves precisely aiming a beam of high-energy X-rays or subatomic particles called protons directly at the tumor. Doctors map the exact location that they want to irradiate prior to the procedure and use a special machine that sends the beam through the skin and to the tumor location. The radiation destroys the DNA in the tumor's cells. Radiation treatment is usually given daily for two to seven weeks, either along with or before or after chemotherapy. It usually takes only a few minutes at a time, but the patient must lie completely still so that the radiation goes only into the tumor. Young children are often sedated during each procedure.

Radiation treatment is more dangerous for young people than for adults. And it is more dangerous for younger children than for older children and teens because it can cause permanent damage to some growing tissues and organs. Its use is limited to situ-

A Combination of Treatments

When Dominic was four months old in 2010, he was diagnosed with glioblastoma, a particularly dangerous and often deadly kind of brain tumor. Doctors first tried to remove the tumor surgically, but it was too big to completely cut out. With the tumor partially removed, the baby then had a course of chemotherapy to shrink the tumor. Once the tumor was small enough, the surgeon operated again and was able to successfully remove it. The danger of remaining cancer cells, however, meant that the boy needed more treatment. Dominic's mother explains, "After the surgery Dominic had to go back on chemo. He had eight cycles in all, over two years. Each cycle was two months." Some of the chemo was so toxic that Dominic's hearing was affected, but the strong drugs were necessary to save his life, even if that meant some hearing loss.

Once his treatment was completed, Dominic was in remission. Nonetheless, for the next five years he returned to the hospital every six months to be sure that he showed no signs of relapse. Finally, in 2016, he was determined to be cancer-free. Today Dominic is a healthy seven-year-old. He still has some hearing loss and wears hearing aids, but he attends a regular school and does well. Dominic beat the odds and survived his cancer thanks to very aggressive treatment.

Ann, "Patient Stories: Dominic's Story," Children with Cancer, February 2017. www.childrenwithcancer.org.uk.

ations in which it is necessary to save patients' lives. The most common temporary side effects are burns to the skin. These burns can be mild, like a sunburn, or painful, but they appear in the days following radiation after repeated daily treatments. The treatment itself causes no pain.

Some tumors do not respond to radiation, but others are very sensitive to it. Radiation therapy is not used for liver cancer or osteosarcoma, but it can be a valuable treatment for Wilms tumors, Ewing sarcomas, neuroblastomas, and soft-tissue sarcomas. Radiation treatments can be used to destroy or shrink tumors or to kill any remaining cancer cells after a tumor has been surgically removed.

Surgery

For all solid tumors, surgery is a critical part of treatment, either before or after chemo or radiation therapy. As Anne Spurgeon and Nancy Keene note, "Surgical removal (called resection) of the primary tumor offers the best chance of a cure for most children diagnosed with a solid tumor."[24] During resection, the pediatric surgeon tries to remove the entire tumor as well as the surrounding tissue to be sure that no cancer cells remain. Sometimes, surgery is all that is required to cure the cancer; usually, though, chemotherapy is given so that any stray cancer cells are destroyed. But sometimes the tumor cannot be completely removed. Some tumors are too large to remove safely. Others are located in hard-to-reach areas of the body. Still other tumors are entwined around organs that the doctor does not want to damage. Often, a large tumor that cannot be removed all at once is first treated with chemo or radiation to shrink it. Once the tumor is small enough, the surgeon can safely remove it. At other times, the surgeon first removes as much of the tumor as he or she can. Then, the patient is treated with chemo or radiation to destroy the rest of the tumor.

> "Surgical removal (called resection) of the primary tumor offers the best chance of a cure for most children diagnosed with a solid tumor."[24]
>
> —Experts Anne Spurgeon and Nancy Keene

Infrequently, cancer surgery involves amputation or complete removal of an organ to remove the cancer and save the patient's life. A child with retinoblastoma, for instance, may have a tumor that has grown so large or has grown into the eye's optic nerve in such a way that the eye and its vision cannot be saved. In that case, a surgeon removes the eye, but the cancer is also removed and the child's life is saved.

Occasionally, a child or teen with osteosarcoma may need a limb amputated to get rid of the cancer. More than 90 percent of the time, however, amputation is not necessary because chemo and surgery can save the arm or leg. Once the surgeon has removed the cancerous parts of the bone, the next task is to use bone grafts and metal devices to restore the remaining bone. These measures ensure that the limb is functional again even though much of the bone had to be removed. But when amputation is necessary above the knee, surgeons can rotate the lower part of the leg and attach it to the femur (thigh bone) in such a way that a substitute knee joint is created. This surgery is called a rotationplasty. After amputation, the lower part of the leg, including the foot, is rotated 180 degrees and is then attached to the femur. The repositioned ankle and foot then act as the new knee joint. The patient is then fitted with a prosthesis that functions as the lower leg and foot. Amputation is the treatment of choice when it is the only way to be sure that the tumor is completely removed.

Targeted Therapy

Surgery, chemotherapy, and radiation cure cancer in most young people, but targeted therapy may help those whose cancer does not respond to standard treatment. Targeted therapy is the use of drugs that specifically attack and kill cancer cells instead of killing all fast-growing cells as chemotherapy does. With some cancers, the genetic and protein changes that cause the cells to become cancerous have been identified. Targeted drugs recognize these changes. Targeted therapy has been developed, for example, for the Philadelphia chromosome. This gene mutation occurs in some cases of ALL and almost all cases of chronic myeloid leukemia (CML), which is a slower-growing form of leukemia in the myeloid cells. Both of these types of leukemia are rare in children, and they can be hard to cure. Often, standard chemotherapy does not work to eliminate the cancer. Targeted drugs that are given in pill form, such as imatinib and dasatinib, attack only cells that carry the Philadelphia chromosome mutation. For

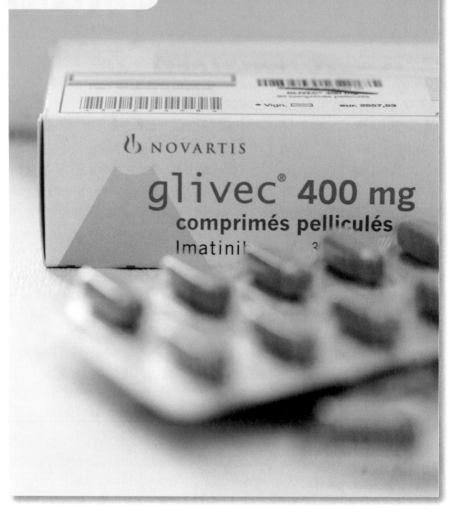

Glivec, or imatinib, is a drug sometimes prescribed to fight leukemia in children. Imatinib targets cancerous cells, leaving healthy cells unaffected.

children with CML, the therapy was approved for use in 2011; for those with ALL, it was approved along with standard chemotherapy in 2013. Use of targeted therapy is so new that doctors cannot yet say whether the drugs lead to a cure. However, most CML patients have experienced long periods of remission and have remained healthy. Children with ALL related to the Philadelphia chromosome mutation also do well. In one study, 70 percent remained disease-free after four years.

Few targeted therapies for cancer in young people have been developed, but research is ongoing to identify the specific gene mutations in cancer that can be targeted. Someday, researchers hope to match the therapy to the genetic mutation of each type of cancer tumor in each individual child or teen. For example, medical researchers are working to identify the genetic changes in brain and spinal cord tumors in children. Some of these mutations have already been found, and researchers are experimenting with new drugs to attack those changes in clinical trials. Clinical trials are studies of new treatments for which people can volunteer. If a child or young person has a cancer that is not responding to standard treatments, he or she may become part of a clinical trial. Not all trials are successful, but sometimes such studies can make a big difference in the fight against cancer.

Immunotherapy

It was a clinical trial of an immunotherapy, for example, that saved Emily Whitehead's life in 2012. Immunotherapy is treatment that uses the body's immune system to fight cancer. Cancer is normally able to hide from the disease-fighting cells of the immune system. With immunotherapy, doctors alter the immune system so that it recognizes cancer as a disease and mounts an attack. Seven-year-old Emily had ALL, and her B cells had become cancerous. She was one of the 10 percent of children with ALL for whom standard cancer treatments do not work. Her cancer relapsed twice, despite two rounds of intense chemotherapy. At that point, Emily, her parents, and her doctors decided to enroll her in a clinical trial at the Children's Hospital of Philadelphia. The trial studied a new immunotherapy known as CAR-T cell therapy.

Emily was the first child ever treated with the procedure. Doctors extracted T cells (the disease-killing white blood cells of the immune system) from Emily's blood. Her T cells were sent to the lab, where a harmless virus inserted a new gene into the cells. The gene reprogrammed the T cells to chemically recognize leukemia cells. B cells have a protein on their surfaces called CD19. Emily's reprogrammed T cells now were able to attach to CD19 and kill the cells. The T cells were multiplied in the lab and then infused back into Emily's body. Although Emily temporarily got very sick as her T cells ferociously attacked the cancer cells, within three weeks she was in remission, with no evidence of disease. In 2017 she passed the five-year mark of being cancer-free. Also in 2017, CAR-T cell therapy was approved by the US government for use in children with ALL not cured by standard therapy.

Toward Future Cures

Medical researchers are studying the use of immunotherapy in more clinical trials as they identify the proteins on the surface of different kinds of cancer cells and develop methods to specifically target those proteins. For children and teens with cancers that do not respond to standard treatments, there is much hope for the future.

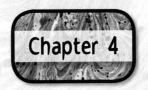

Chapter 4

What Is It Like to Live with Cancer?

L iving with cancer can be difficult from the moment of diagnosis, throughout treatment, and even after the cancer is in remission. It can be physically and emotionally draining and affect all aspects of a young person's life. Cancer also can impact the whole family and affect relationships with family and friends. Nevertheless, most young people with cancer figure out how to fight and how to live normal, optimistic lives.

Confronting Diagnosis

Living with cancer begins immediately at diagnosis, often with a feeling of shock and disbelief. Alfie, who was diagnosed with acute lymphoblastic leukemia (ALL), explains: "The feeling of being told that news is like no other. It's a mixture of sadness, fear, anger and confusion all bundled together in a frenzy of disbelief."[25] Many teens describe similar reactions to the terrible moment when they learned they had cancer. *Cancer* is a frightening word.

Clarissa Schilstra clearly remembers when she heard the doctor's diagnosis of leukemia when she was thirteen. She says, "Life as you know it suddenly stops, and you are left to wonder if it is all real. All that ran through my head during the following hours was, 'Could this really be happening to me?'" Clarissa and her parents were together when the doctor gave them the news, and she also remembers watching their reaction.

Clarissa may have felt numb—even when the doctor said her chance of survival was only 40 percent, it did not sink in—but her parents were crying and consumed with grief. The girl felt more worried about her parents than about herself, and her powerlessness to make things better for them hurt her. She says now, "In some way, I think it is important for others to remember that, in the moment of diagnosis, you are not only thinking of your own world, you are thinking of how this will affect your friends and family."[26]

Clarissa was admitted to the hospital immediately, and chemo began that night, only hours after her diagnosis. The rapid medical response was necessary because her cancer cells had already spread to her spinal fluid, and her best chance of survival lay in an intense treatment plan to destroy the aggressively spreading leukemia. Then the reality of the danger set in, and Clarissa was scared, angry, and sad. Still, she would not let herself think about dying. Instead, she was determined to "get ready to do whatever it would take"[27] to win out over the cancer. She was determined not to let her disease ruin the lives of her parents, her friends, or anyone who loved her. She would regain control of her life and survive. She became stoical and intent upon fighting to be healthy again, no matter what she had to endure.

Everyone reacts to a diagnosis of cancer differently, often depending upon his or her age or personality. Today Clarissa thinks she acted so strong about it because she was refusing to face the danger she might be in. Some people do not let themselves think about what the future holds. Others may focus on a small part of what cancer means to them. One teen's first thought, for example, was worry that he would lose his hair. Hair loss also worried fourteen-year-old Lily when she was diagnosed. The British teen remembers:

> At first, when I was told I had Hodgkin's lymphoma I didn't react at all because I had no idea what they were talking about. I didn't even think young people got cancer, not teenagers anyway. I thought it was just old people and little kids, not people my age. Then when I realised it really was cancer, it was like everything went into slow motion and I went into shock. I only really reacted when the doctor said I would lose my hair and also couldn't go on the holiday we had planned for the following week—that's when I started to cry.[28]

Cancer undoubtedly hampers the health of young victims, but it can be emotionally devastating as well. Those affected will experience fear and anger, and many can also be overwhelmed by treatment options.

The Fear of Death

At other times, however, young people are simply afraid. Avamarie, for instance, was nine years old when she was diagnosed with a cancerous kidney tumor (Wilms tumor) that had spread to her lungs. Her mother, Desiree George, broke the news to her after meeting with the child's doctors. George sat down beside her daughter and said, "The doctors have found a big lump on your tummy. It is making you sick, so they have to make it smaller with medicine, and then they are going to take it out. Do you know what the name for it is?" Her mother was trying to break the news gently, but Avamarie immediately understood. She asked, "'Mum, do I have cancer? Am I going to die?"[29]

The fear of death and dying is a normal, natural response to learning one has cancer. Many people have some familiarity with

When Treatment Fails

Sometimes, young people with cancer do not survive, despite the best efforts of the medical world. Zach Sobiech was diagnosed with osteosarcoma at age fourteen. Although doctors aggressively treated his cancer with several surgeries and rounds of chemotherapy, the cancer metastasized to his lungs and pelvis. In 2012, when he was eighteen, doctors told Zach that they could not help him and had no more treatments to offer. Zach made the decision to live as fully and happily as he could for as much time as he had left. He was a musician, and he wrote a song called "Clouds" to say good-bye to his friends and family and all his fans. Zach and his family also set up the Zach Sobiech Osteosarcoma Fund in partnership with the Children's Cancer Research Fund. Its goal is to support research into new and better treatments for osteosarcoma, and the organization continues to grow. Zach accomplished a lot during his life and left an enduring legacy. He once explained, "I want to be remembered as the kid who went down fighting, and didn't really lose." He died on May 20, 2013.

Zach Sobiech Osteosarcoma Fund, "Zach's Story, and the Clouds' Silver Lining," Children's Cancer Research Fund. https://childrenscancer.org.

cancer. Perhaps older relatives have died from the disease, or they have seen depictions of cancer in books and movies or on television. It can take time after a diagnosis for hope to return and to experience the encouragement that vigorous medical treatment brings. Toby, who was diagnosed at age fifteen, remembers, "The world around me simply froze as the consultant at the hospital uttered that I had Leukaemia—cancer of the blood. My first thought after hearing Leukaemia was my Grandad who had been diagnosed twenty years prior and subsequently died from the illness; I believed I awaited the same fate."[30]

> "Mum, do I have cancer? Am I going to die?"[29]
>
> —Avamarie, a cancer patient

When a very young child is diagnosed with cancer, he or she may not understand, but parents and older siblings do. They are the ones who fear the disease and worry about the child's survival. Courtney, for instance, was eighteen months old when she was diagnosed, and it was her parents and ten-year-old brother, Jay, who were scared. Jay asked their mother if Courtney was going to die. Their mother, who was terrified herself, recalls, "I ached to lie to him and tell him that everything would be all right. I wanted to say, 'Of course she isn't,' but I couldn't do it. . . . I told him his sister might die, but that we were going to do everything we could to make sure that didn't happen."[31]

The fear of death never completely goes away. Yet as treatment gets under way, people with cancer and their families learn to adjust to their new reality and to cope with a new way of living. Fifteen-year-old Lexie, who has undergone treatment several times for cancer and subsequent relapses, believes attitude matters more than anything. "My advice to any teen that has just been diagnosed is to live life like nothing is going on," she says. "The biggest piece of advice I can give is to have a good attitude and try to live life to the best of your ability because later on you will regret all the opportunities you passed up."[32]

Hospitalization

Such advice sometimes can be hard to follow, especially at the start of treatment. But with courage and determination, people like Lexie can learn to live with cancer. Spending time in a hospital is the first major adjustment that young people with cancer must make. Hospitals can seem like scary, painful places. People must get used to frequent needle pokes for medicine, blood draws, and testing; repeated exposure to medical devices and machines; and constant visits and checkups from medical staff.

> "I felt like I was stuck in time, waiting for what seemed like forever, to finish my treatment."[33]
>
> —Cancer survivor Clarissa Schilstra

Children and teens sometimes experience prolonged hospital stays, perhaps for months at a time. And, even when they can stay at home, they are required to go back to the hospital, perhaps even daily, for treatment and testing. Many people say that the hospital becomes a second home. Long absences from normal life, such as school and time with friends, are common. At times, long stays in the hospital are just plain boring and lonely. Many favorite activities are no longer possible.

When Clarissa was cancer-free and a senior in college, she wrote an advice book for teens living with cancer. In the book, she discusses what life was like during cancer treatments:

> As you will unfortunately come to know, hospital rooms get very lonely. . . . You may spend weeks or months in that room, rarely leaving. Those long days cooped up in a small space can take their toll emotionally. When you finally get to go home, it is not always much better. There may be the comforts of everything you know and your family who loves you, but being stuck at home in bed or on the couch can sometimes feel like a jail cell from which you cannot escape. . . . I felt like I was stuck in time, waiting for what seemed like forever, to finish my treatment. It seemed like everyone around me was moving on, growing up and enjoying life.[33]

Teens may also have particular difficulty adjusting to the lack of control they feel during hospitalization and treatment. At a time of life when they most want to be independent and make their own choices, they must turn that control over to doctors and nurses and depend on others to make decisions for them and control most aspects of their lives. Dependency becomes their new normal. Toby comments, "I was stripped of my independence, dignity and adolescence."[34]

Many young people living with cancer must visit hospitals and treatment centers routinely, sometimes spending days or weeks in clinical settings. Doctors and nurses become like family, helping to make the experience as comforting as possible.

Despite all the negatives, most young people find ways to make life in the hospital as normal as possible. Clarissa brought from home everything she could think of to make her hospital stays more comfortable. She decorated her hospital room with cards and ribbons. She brought her favorite pillows, blankets, movies, and games. Other teens hang posters, photographs, or pictures on the walls or windows. They carry their video games and tablets with them for every hospital stay. They turn their hospital rooms into homes, and the staff, especially the nurses, become new family members. Almost every young person with cancer mentions the nurses as the best part of the hospital. Nurses often become good friends, confidants, and sources of ongoing encouragement and support.

Trying for Normal

Specialized children's cancer treatment hospitals also make a strong effort to provide children and teens with activities and happy experiences. In the special cancer units of Britain's Teenage Cancer Trust, for example, where Toby and Alfie were treated, visiting hours are long and flexible so that patients can maintain contacts with friends and family. The staff offers social activities within the hospital, fun outings away from the hospital for those who are able to participate, and even massages and relaxation therapies to help people feel comfortable. Parents, who usually accompany their children, can stay with the patients and have their own lounge available. At the University of Michigan's C.S. Mott Children's Hospital, where Lexie was treated, patients are offered pizza and live entertainment every Thursday night. The hospital also has music and art therapy programs. Many hospitals have media libraries where parents and patients can check out movies and DVDs, and most have Internet access so kids can stay connected with friends through social media or play computer games.

Hard for Everyone

Brothers and sisters of a young person with cancer must learn to live with cancer too. In practical terms, they often have to live with little attention from parents and other family members when all the concern and attention turn to the child with cancer. They may have to struggle with their own fear and grief with little support from others. They may get angry and resentful, yet feel guilty about being concerned for their own needs. Zach Sobiech's older sister Alli, for example, felt horrible about herself as she watched her younger brother dying of cancer. She remembers wanting everything to be over because she and her other siblings wanted life to get better again. At the same time, she felt awful for wishing her brother would die because she desperately loved him and did not want him to die at all. She was relieved to learn from a social worker that her feelings were normal and she was not a terrible person.

Clarissa Schilstra, on the other hand, remembers how hard her cancer treatment was for her younger brother. She tried hard to protect him from the knowledge of what she was going through during treatment, and she felt guilty about how neglected he often was. After Clarissa's treatment was over, her brother told her, "I felt like the only child of divorced parents." He was lonely, worried, and lacking much support. The whole family had to work to feel normal again after Clarissa recovered.

Quoted in Clarissa Schilstra, *Riding the Cancer Coaster: Survival Guide for Teens and Young Adults.* Seattle: Amazon Digital Services, October 24, 2015. Kindle edition.

Almost all specialized pediatric cancer centers have playrooms for younger children that are well equipped with toys, such as blocks, dolls, and cars, as well as with books and games. Often, child life specialists are available in playrooms to play with the children, and children can mingle with other children there too. When patients are confined to their rooms, perhaps because the risk of infection is too great to be around others or perhaps because they are too weak and sick to leave their beds, music and art therapists will come to them. Some hospitals have closed-circuit television and offer things like televised bingo games for patients confined to bed to enjoy. One mother remembers the fun of recreation therapy for her daughter Katy. The recreation therapist came to Katy's room when Katy's mother needed a break to talk with a doctor. The therapist played with Katy while her mother was gone. "Katy had a great time making herself a gold crown and decorating her wheelchair with streamers and jewels,"[35] her mom remembers.

For patients who are missing out on normal school life, St. Jude Children's Research Hospital has its own classrooms and teachers to help kids keep up with their classes. It holds graduation ceremonies for kindergarteners and high school students who must miss their own graduation ceremonies at home. Every spring, St. Jude even has a prom for teens between the ages of thirteen and nineteen who cannot go to their proms at home. The young people can wear gowns and tuxedos and have stylists come in to fix their makeup and hair.

Enduring Cancer Treatment

Hospitals provide young cancer patients with fun diversions so they can experience as much normal life as possible. Yet no amount of pleasurable activity can change the fact that living with cancer is sometimes physically miserable and emotionally stressful. Sometimes people are just too sick to care about normal life. Living with cancer means living with cancer treatments, and often that means just enduring. As seven-year-old Stephan explains, "We've got to do it, so let's just get it done."[36]

Young people living with cancer treatment, no matter what their ages, echo that sentiment. They know the treatment is necessary to kill their cancer and cure them, so they endure the nausea, weakness and tiredness, and other side effects that are so often the inevitable result of chemo or radiation. They endure the isolation that their weakened immune systems require. And they cope with the pain of surgeries or other procedures that are often a part of treatment. They exhibit courage and determination, no

A music therapist helps keep up the spirits of a teenage cancer patient in a Sacramento, California, medical center. Such facilities have learned that young cancer patients need diversions and fun to keep them from focusing solely on the disease and its treatments.

matter how long it takes. "I have learned to accept the fact that I have Cancer," seventeen-year-old Celeste writes. "And I want to get through this therapy."[37] Fifteen-year-old Jacob agrees. "Always keep your head up!"[38] he encourages. And fourteen-year-old Tamia offers this advice: "It may be hard, but if you believe in yourself and don't give up, you'll make it through. You're stronger than any illness."[39]

Of course, no one can have such a positive attitude all the time. Everyone has days when they are angry or sad or tired of fighting. Very young children, for instance, may have temper tantrums and not really understand why. Older children and teens suffer through days when they cry or just want to sleep all the time or need encouragement and reassurance from staff and parents to keep going.

Different people have different ways of finding the strength to go through cancer treatment and still maintain hope for the future. Some find that friends make all the difference. Lexie, for instance, had good friends who vowed to always remain friends, offered her sympathy and comfort, and really worked to include her in their activities when she was able. She also tried hard herself to be a happy person. She says, "Here's the thing, cancer sucks and we all know it so instead of wasting the little energy I have left pouting and throwing myself a pity party, why not smile and try to enjoy life a little."[40] Clarissa, too, relied on friends, but she also depended on her parents to get her through the bad times. When she was at her most helpless, she realized that she could always trust and count on them to help her and stand up for her, whether she needed a different medicine for nausea or a shoulder to cry on. She feels that her cancer brought her and her parents closer together.

Many young people with cancer also rely on their faith to make sense of their experiences. Shannon, for example, was twelve years old when she finished two years of treatment for her cancerous tumor. Finally healthy and back to school and a normal life, she reflects that

> having cancer stinks! Having chemo stinks even more! However, God has a plan for everyone and His plan was for me to have a tumor. His plan was for me to have chemo for two years. I don't understand why but I have faith that God knows what He is doing and I hope I am done with being sick. I thank God for putting so many wonderful people in the path of my chemo journey.[41]

Treatment's End

When treatment finally comes to an end and the cancer is gone, young survivors begin to move forward with their lives. Many have end-of-chemo parties to celebrate. Fifteen-year-old Carly, for instance, was delighted when her cancer treatment was over and she could get back to normal life, despite the need to return to her doctors for regular checkups. Still, she remembers, "When I left the hospital I was nervous. I hadn't been in the real world in a while. But I realized it gets better. Things go back to normal eventually. You'll be able to look back on it and be done with it."[42]

Some young people put their cancer journey in the past right away and dive back into normal life. Others worry every time they go back for a checkup to be sure the cancer is still in remission, which they will do for five years. Some have trouble adjusting to normal life after spending so much time as a cancer patient. And still others feel that their cancer experience helped them to grow and become better people. Cynthia Sekerke, for example, is an adult now, but looking back at her cancer journey at age sixteen, she says,

> I don't think I would wish childhood cancer on anyone. . . . [But] I really can't say I'm sorry that it happened. Because the things that happened in my life were most definitely for a reason. And I may not know all of those reasons today. Nothing happens accidentally. I have seen the fact that I've been able to come alongside people and I think be a benefit to them because I know what they're feeling.[43]

It can take years to put the cancer experience in perspective, and most young people have some trouble at first. One college freshman who had cancer at age fifteen describes the difficulties of facing and dealing with all the emotions that cancer can evoke. This survivor says, "I tried so hard as a freshman in college to put it all behind me and get on with my life. It just didn't work. . . . I had nightmares every night. I'd wake up feeling that I had needles in my arms."[44] It took a while and some therapy with a counselor to get over all the bad memories of cancer treatment.

Cancer Conquerors

Living with cancer can be a traumatic experience. Like a soldier coming home from war, survivors may be left with feelings of anxiety or even post-traumatic stress disorder. Clarissa says, "In fact, I think patients are soldiers, just on a different battlefield. They fight for their lives, against their own bodies, and experience life-changing traumas. The battle can rage on for months and years. Then, one day, your treatment is just done. You are supposed to go home and start a normal life again."[45] But it can take time to learn to live *without* cancer too. Remarkably, that is exactly what most young people do as they put cancer behind them. They truly are warriors, who fight and win.

Source Notes

Introduction: A Once-Deadly Disease

1. Quoted in Malcolm Gladwell, "The Treatment: Why Is It So Difficult to Develop Drugs for Cancer?," *New Yorker*, May 17, 2010. www.newyorker.com.
2. G. Bennett Humphrey, *Breaking Little Bones: Triumph and Trauma, the First Cures of Childhood Leukemia*. Seattle: Amazon Digital Services, 2016. Kindle edition.
3. Jessica Burkhamer, David Kriebel, and Richard Clapp, "The Increasing Toll of Adolescent Cancer Incidence in the US," *PLOS One,* February 24, 2017. http://journals.plos.org.
4. St. Jude Children's Research Hospital, "Why Support Us?" www.stjude.org.

Chapter 1: What Is Cancer?

5. American Association for Cancer Research, "What Is Cancer?" www.aacrfoundation.org.
6. Quoted in Trisha Paul, ed., *Chronicling Childhood Cancer: A Collection of Personal Stories by Children and Teens with Cancer.* Ann Arbor: MPublishing, University of Michigan Library, 2015, p. 75.
7. Quoted in Anne Spurgeon and Nancy Keene, *Childhood Cancer: A Parent's Guide to Solid Tumor Cancers,* 3rd ed. Bellingham, WA: Childhood Cancer Guides, 2016, p. 13.

8. Quoted in Spurgeon and Keene, *Childhood Cancer*, p. 74.

9. Quoted in Spurgeon and Keene, *Childhood Cancer*, p. 76.

10. Lily, "Young People's Stories: Lily, Suffolk," Teenage Cancer Trust. www.teenagecancertrust.org.

Chapter 2: What Causes Cancer?

11. Quoted in Paul, ed., *Chronicling Childhood Cancer*, p. 13.

12. Quoted in Spurgeon and Keene, *Childhood Cancer*, pp. 4–5.

13. American Cancer Society, "Risk Factors and Causes of Childhood Cancer," August 22, 2016. www.cancer.org.

14. Spurgeon and Keene, *Childhood Cancer*, p. 5.

15. National Cancer Institute, "Common Cancer Myths and Misconceptions," February 3, 2014. www.cancer.gov.

16. National Cancer Institute, "The Genetics of Cancer," October 12, 2017. www.cancer.gov.

17. American Cancer Society, "Genes and Cancer: Changes in Genes," June 25, 2014. www.cancer.org.

18. American Cancer Society, "Genes and Cancer: Oncogenes and Tumor Suppressor Genes," June 25, 2014. www.cancer.org.

19. St. Jude Children's Research Hospital, "St. Jude–Washington University Pediatric Cancer Genome Project." www.stjude.org.

Chapter 3: Can Cancer Be Treated or Cured?

20. Children's Cancer Institute, "Childhood Cancer: The Facts." https://ccia.org.au.

21. National Cancer Institute, "Childhood Acute Lymphoblastic Leukemia Treatment (PDQ)–Patient Version," October 26, 2017. www.cancer.gov.

22. American Cancer Society, "Cancer in Children: Treating Children with Cancer," August 22, 2016. www.cancer.org.

23. Clarissa Schilstra, *Riding the Cancer Coaster: Survival Guide for Teens and Young Adults.* Seattle: Amazon Digital Services, October 24, 2015. Kindle edition.

24. Spurgeon and Keene, *Childhood Cancer,* p. 202.

Chapter 4: What Is It Like to Live with Cancer?

25. Alfie, "Young People's Stories: Alfie, Suffolk," Teenage Cancer Trust. www.teenagecancertrust.org.

26. Schilstra, *Riding the Cancer Coaster*.

27. Schilstra, *Riding the Cancer Coaster*.

28. Lily, "Young People's Stories."

29. Quoted in Annemarie Quill, "'Mum, Do I Have Cancer? Am I Going to Die?," *New Zealand Herald*, June 4, 2017. www.nzherald.co.nz.

30. Toby, "Young People's Stories: Toby, Stratford-Upon-Avon," Teenage Cancer Trust. www.teenagecancertrust.org.

31. Quoted in Spurgeon and Keene, *Childhood Cancer*, p. 354.

32. Quoted in Paul, ed., *Chronicling Childhood Cancer*, p. 7.

33. Schilstra*, Riding the Cancer Coaster*.

34. Toby, "Young People's Stories."

35. Quoted in Spurgeon and Keene, *Childhood Cancer,* p. 180.

36. Quoted in Spurgeon and Keene, *Childhood Cancer,* p. 355.

37. Quoted in Paul, ed., *Chronicling Childhood Cancer,* p. 39.

38. Quoted in Paul, ed*., Chronicling Childhood Cancer,* p. 49.

39. Quoted in Paul, ed*., Chronicling Childhood Cancer,* p. 53.

40. Quoted in Paul, ed., *Chronicling Childhood Cancer*, p. 6.

41. Quoted in Paul, ed., *Chronicling Childhood Cancer*, p. 6.

42. Quoted in Children's Hospital of Philadelphia, "Acute Myelogenous Leukemia: Carly's Story," September 2012. www.chop.edu.

43. Quoted in Stephanie Kuo, "Stories of Survivors of Childhood Cancer," KERA News, March 3, 2015. http://stories.kera .org.
44. Quoted in Spurgeon and Keene, *Childhood Cancer,* p. 352.
45. Schilstra, *Riding the Cancer Coaster*.

American Cancer Society

250 Williams St. NW
Atlanta, GA 30303
website: www.cancer.org

With services and offices in every state, the American Cancer Society also maintains an extensive website, with information on every kind of cancer, support services, and resources for education and research. It offers a special section on childhood cancer.

American Childhood Cancer Organization

6868 Distribution Dr.
Beltsville, MD 20705
website: www.acco.org

This group of families, survivors, and friends advocates to make childhood and teen cancer a national health priority. It offers support to those affected by childhood cancer, as well as information, education, and advocacy. On its website, it provides many resources for children, teens, and parents dealing with cancer.

Leukemia & Lymphoma Society

3 International Dr., Suite 200
Rye Brook, NY 10573
website: www.lls.org

Dedicated to supporting research and raising awareness about blood cancers, this organization has a resource center to help people find information and support, access to the latest news about cancer research breakthroughs, and an online peer-to-peer support group for those newly diagnosed.

National Cancer Institute (NCI)

9609 Medical Center Dr.
BG 9609 MSC 9760
Bethesda, MD 20892
website: www.cancer.gov

A division of the National Institutes of Health, the NCI offers a wide array of cancer information. It is also the source for information on the latest cancer clinical trials.

St. Jude Children's Research Hospital

262 Danny Thomas Pl.
Memphis, TN 38105
website: www.stjude.org

St. Jude maintains an extensive website with information about current cancer research, treatment options for children, and stories about families dealing with cancer.

Teen Cancer America

11835 Olympic Blvd., #265 E
Los Angeles, CA 90064
website: www.teencanceramerica.org

This nonprofit organization is dedicated specifically to teens with cancer and their treatment. It works with hospitals and outpatient clinics to provide support and education about the needs of teens. It offers a section with many teen and young adult stories about dealing with cancer.

For Further Research

Books

John Allen, *The Importance of Cell Theory*. San Diego: Reference-Point, 2015.

Karen Bush Gibson, *Cells: Experience Life at Its Tiniest*. White River Junction, VT: Nomad, 2017.

Paul Klenerman, *The Immune System: A Very Short Introduction*. New York: Oxford University Press, 2017.

Siva Ganesh Maharaja, *Cancer Information for Teens*. 4th ed. Detroit: Omnigraphics, 2018.

Meg Marquardt, *Curing Cancer*. Mankato, MN: 12 Story Library, 2017.

Internet Sources

American Cancer Society, "Cancer in Adolescents." www.cancer.org/cancer/cancer-in-adolescents.html.

American Society of Clinical Oncology, "Childhood Cancer," Cancer.Net. www.cancer.net/cancer-types/childhood-cancer.

Children's Hospital of Philadelphia, "Brain Tumors Patient Stories." www.chop.edu/conditions-diseases/pediatric-brain-tumors/patient-stories.

KidsHealth, "What Is Cancer?" http://kidshealth.org/en/kids/can cer.html.

LiveStrong, "Young Adults with Cancer." https://www.livestrong .org/we-can-help/just-diagnosed/young-adults-with-cancer.

St. Baldrick's Foundation, "Pediatric Cancer Research Facts: A Decade of Successes," *St. Baldrick's Foundation Blog,* February 22, 2016. www.stbaldricks.org/blog/post/pediatric-cancer-re search-facts-a-decade-of-successes-infographic.

Index

Picture Credits

Cover: XiXiinXing/iStockphoto.com

6: Madeline Gray/Zuma Press/Newscom

10: Steve Gschmeissner/Science Source

13: Maury Aaseng

17: Simon Fraser/Science Source

25: LiquidLibrary/Thinkstock Images

28: Biophoto Associates/Science Source

33: National Cancer Institute/Science Source

38: Maury Aaseng

42: Joe Burbank/KRT/Newscom

48: Véronique Burger/Science Source

53: iStock/Thinkstock Images

57: Karen Pulfer Focht/Zuma Press/Newscom

61: Renee C. Byer/Zuma Press/Newscom

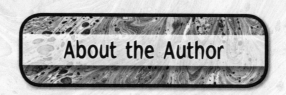

oney Allman holds degrees from Ohio State University and the University of Hawaii. She currently lives in Virginia, where she enjoys a rural lifestyle as well as researching and writing about a variety of topics for students.